PSYCHOPATHIA SEXUALIS

BY
JOHN PATRICK SHANLEY

★

★

DRAMATISTS
PLAY SERVICE
INC.

2

PSYCHOPATHIA SEXUALIS was produced by Manhattan Theatre Club (Lynne Meadow, Artistic Director; Barry Grove, Managing Director) in New York City, on February 26, 1997. It was directed by Daniel Sullivan; the set design was by Derek McLane; the costume design was by Jane Greenwood; the lighting design was by Pat Collins; the sound design was by John Kilgore; and the production stage manager was Michael Brunner. The cast was as follows:

ELLIE	Margaret Colin
HOWARD	Daniel Gerroll
ARTHUR	Andrew McCarthy
DR. BLOCK	Edward Herrmann
LUCILLE	Park Overall

PSYCHOPATHIA SEXUALIS was produced by Center Theatre Group at Mark Taper Forum (Gordon Davidson, Artistic Director; Charles Dillingham, Managing Director; Robert Egan, Producing Director) in Los Angeles, California, on May 22, 1996. It was directed by Daniel Sullivan; the set design was by Andrew Wood Boughton; the costume design was by Jane Greenwood; the lighting design was by Pat Collins; the sound design was by Steven M. Klein; and the production stage manager was Mary Michele Miner. The cast was as follows:

ELLIE	Talia Balsam
HOWARD	Gregory Itzin
ARTHUR	Matt Servitto
DR. BLOCK	John Aylward
LUCILLE	Park Overall

PSYCHOPATHIA SEXUALIS was produced by Seattle Repertory Theater (Daniel Sullivan, Artistic Director; Benjamin Moore, Managing Director) in Seattle, Washington, on March 13, 1996. It was directed by Daniel Sullivan; the set design was by Andrew Wood Boughton; the costume design was by Jane Greenwood; the lighting design was by Pat Collins; the sound design was by Steven M. Klein; and the stage manager was Karen Quisenberry. The cast was as follows:

ELLIE ....Talia Balsam
HOWARD ....Daniel Sullivan
ARTHUR...Matt Servitto
DR. BLOCK ....John Aylward
LUCILLE ....Park Overall

PSYCHOPATHIA SEXUALIS

ACT ONE

Scene 1

Ellie, in a chic dressing gown, is sitting at a breakfast table, drinking her coffee and writing on a pad. A cheerful rock-and-roll song is playing on a stereo. Howard enters in his bathrobe with his newspaper. He is English. He takes in the scene and calls out:

HOWARD.   Controls. *(Ellie hands him a remote control. He immediately clicks off the music, pours himself coffee, and starts to read the paper.)*
ELLIE.   I was listening to that.
HOWARD.   So was I. And there we have the dilemma of marriage.
ELLIE.   Good morning, Howard.
HOWARD.   Good morning, Ellie.
ELLIE.   You've been preoccupied.
HOWARD.   I don't think so.
ELLIE.   Cranky.
HOWARD.   I have my sensitivities. For instance, now I'm trying to read the *Wall Street Journal.*
ELLIE.   The *Journal!* I thought you'd sworn off?
HOWARD.   Nothing is forever.
ELLIE.   Sleep well?
HOWARD.   Reasonably.
ELLIE.   Are you having an affair?
HOWARD.   What! No!
ELLIE.   Just checking.
HOWARD.   Talk show tactics.

5

ELLIE.   Sorry. I smell a problem and I'm a problem solver.

HOWARD.   What's that you're writing there?

ELLIE.   I'm taking a course at The New School. Creative writing.

HOWARD.   Well. I suppose it's better than destructive writing. Always trying to improve yourself.

ELLIE.   Or you.

HOWARD.   You try to improve me?

ELLIE.   Oh, you're my project.

HOWARD.   Am I? How am I going?

ELLIE.   There's something on your mind.

HOWARD.   How do you know that?

ELLIE.   You're a column of numbers. I add them up. One is missing.

HOWARD.   Not exactly flattering. My husband the deficit.

ELLIE.   So? Are there beans to spill?

HOWARD.   I don't care to share. What kind of thing are you writing?

ELLIE.   A poem.

HOWARD.   A poem! Poetry. You?

ELLIE.   We're supposed to mimic an assigned poet.

HOWARD.   Who were you assigned? Omar the tent maker?

ELLIE.   Kipling. Rudyard Kipling.

HOWARD.   The jingoist? I wouldn't think he'd suit you.

ELLIE.   I don't mind him.

HOWARD.   "And if you can keep your lunch, when all about you are losing theirs...." So what did you write?

ELLIE.   Just a, you know, it's a little fictional ditty.

HOWARD.   Read it.

ELLIE.   It's fictional.

HOWARD.   Read the fiction.

ELLIE.

> When my mother was a mother
> Her course was set
> Or so it seemed to me
> First you beguile
> And then you beget
> And then you're a family

HOWARD.   Very nice.

ELLIE.

> But as I make my way
> Through capricious seas
> 'Cross the nights and days of now
> What seemed so right
> Has spun from sight
> I cannot answer how

HOWARD.   It's getting darker,

ELLIE.   I could stop.

HOWARD.   No, don't stop.

ELLIE.

> I'm a trophy wife
> A second wife
> A spouse in the house of show
> How I came to this
> Through a careless kiss
> I really do not know
>
> But do not disregard me
> As a decorative green card joke
> Though my marriage springs
> From ridiculous things
> It's turned out okedoke

That's as far as I got.

HOWARD.   Thank god. Fiction, huh?

ELLIE.   Not a word of truth in it.

HOWARD.   Sometimes I don't think I know you.

ELLIE.   Sometimes I don't think I know you.

HOWARD.   You were right before. There is something on my mind. But to tell you would certainly be a betrayal of trust.

ELLIE.   Oh come on! What's marriage for?

HOWARD.   It will go no further?

ELLIE.   *Apres moi, le Deluge.*

HOWARD.   Stop it. French. All right. Last Saturday.… The dinner party was over.… Well, let me set the scene. You'd excused yourself and gone to bed.

ELLIE.   Goodnight. *(Ellie exits. Howard speaks after her, as if she's*

7

still there. He has picked up the stereo control.)

HOWARD.   The room still smelled of your fabulous osso bucco. *(The lights change, Arthur enters, and sits in the indicated chair. Howard takes off his bathrobe and he's fully dressed.)* I had the fire going. Arthur was sitting in the slipper chair, and I was playing him a piece of music. *(Howard clicks on the music and conducts the finale of Beethoven's* Ninth* *with great commitment. He's moved down into the hearth area. A fire is burning in the invisible fireplace. Arthur is sitting in the slipper chair. Howard, when he sits, will sit in a wing chair.)* Nine times, but he finally got it right. My father's god. Ludwig van Beethoven.

ARTHUR.   That was your father's favorite part of the symphony?

HOWARD.   Always. The climax. That was IT for him.

ARTHUR.   Yes. My father believed in guilt. He'd say, you have to *earn* a climax.

HOWARD.   My father believed in results. Even when he read the Bible. He always turned right to the Apocalypse.

ARTHUR.   Revelations. Speaking of which.

HOWARD.   We must drink. This was a gift from Ellie. A very good single malt.

ARTHUR.   None for me, thanks.

HOWARD.   The glasses are Japanese. They've got an incredible tactility. Just feel this glass.

ARTHUR.   You're such a salesman.

HOWARD.   Oh, come on, have a taste. To make more temperate the vexatious climate of a troubled age.

ARTHUR.   All right, but just a taste. I'm on a bit of a health kick. I mean I'm trying to get up a show and …

HOWARD.   Anyway, this is sort've the best part of the evening, isn't it? Good dinner, fire, a drink. Get to talk about, you know, moonlight.

ARTHUR.   Moonlight. There's a topic …

HOWARD.   This is intimacy! This is real intimacy!

ARTHUR.   This is? Oh good. Good.

HOWARD.   So, you're working hard, huh?

* See Special Note on Songs and Recordings on copyright page.

8

ARTHUR.   Well, I've been trying to put up a show, as I said. The gallery's being very nice about it, but.... Look, I don't want to talk about work.

HOWARD.   Well, you know, that's fine with me. I hate work.

ARTHUR.   You're the hardest working guy who hates work I've ever met.

HOWARD.   Not now.

ARTHUR.   This is good Scotch. Who's running the Fund now?

HOWARD.   Jerry somebody. He calls me, you know. He gets nervous. It's a lot of money to manage and he's terrified he might blow it. He won't. But you don't want to talk about work, and I certainly don't want to talk about money. The pursuit of money is a carcinogenic lunacy.

ARTHUR.   It's amazing how you changed your life.

HOWARD.   Is it? Even bugs can metamorphasize.

ARTHUR.   But to give up such an important job.

HOWARD.   It wasn't that important.

ARTHUR.   Was it hard to give up?

HOWARD.   No. That job was part of an external reality. My real journey began afterward. You know we took that cruise. Three months. After a few days at sea, I got frantic. It was like I was being attacked by a swarm of bees. I started writing these notes. Different ideas for what to do with the rest of my life. I wrote six hundred pages of notes in three weeks.

ARTHUR.   Jesus.

HOWARD.   Then I started screaming at Ellie. Just mad abuse. Really angry. She was.... She fought me, you know. On whatever demented point I happened to be making. Then she realized it was just.... That this was just an outpouring, that there was no point in trying to stop it. So she took aerobics. Then the nightmares started. You know, you sleep in this deep, deep way on the ocean. And your dreams, at least my dreams, started to get very big. I dreamed the house I grew up in was gone, and the spot where it had stood was just a scorched black place on the earth. I dreamt that I had murdered someone, and I was racked with guilt and fear of discovery. I dreamt that I had wronged various celebrities, murdered them, stolen from them, lost their children that had been left in my care. I

9

dreamt about you.

ARTHUR. Me?

HOWARD. I dreamt that you were the Fool, and I was King Lear.

ARTHUR. I was...?

HOWARD. And then I had this sort've pivotal dream, where I was a Roman, and a Greek was in charge of me. This Greek was to supervise my suicide. I was supposed to plunge this dagger into my own heart. I was very afraid. I was crying and calling out to God for the courage to kill myself. And in such a difficult, painful way. Why did it have to be so difficult? But the Greek just waited for me, the Roman, to do it. To kill myself.

ARTHUR. Man. What was that about?

HOWARD. Well, I think I know. See, to me, the Greeks were contemplative, artistic, complex. The Romans were simpler, much less artistic though they appreciated art, and pragmatic. Powerful. They conquered the Greeks. They were organizers, administrators, warriors. I think my dream was about my own unbalanced personality. I'd used the Roman side of myself to manage a huge international stock portfolio. To become rich, successful. Powerful in the world of men. But now the Greek side of me, more complex, more contemplative, artistic, was dictating that the Roman in me must make way, step aside. Die. And that's what my anger and anguish and confusion was about on that boat. The Greek in me was supervising the suicide of the Roman in me. And the Roman didn't want to die.

ARTHUR. Did he die?

HOWARD. Sort've.

ARTHUR. I mean, that wouldn't be good would it?

HOWARD. Well he didn't completely die. If he completely died, I'd be horribly imbalanced in a different way. But the Greek is definitely having his day.

ARTHUR. And how come I was the Fool and you were King Lear?

HOWARD. Well, me, Lear, power, power misused. Fall from power. You, the Fool, the wise one. And Art. The Artist. And maybe my only friend.

ARTHUR. We are friends, aren't we? I mean I guess we are

friends.

HOWARD. I don't know, Arthur. I think we are.

ARTHUR. I've got a reason for wanting to know.

HOWARD. I mean, of course, absolutely we are.

ARTHUR. Because I've got it in mind to ask you something. But it's predicated on an assumption of friendship.

HOWARD. Yes. We're friends. We're friends.

ARTHUR. Because I wanted to ask you something. Well, to tell you something, and then ask you something, and then ask you something else.

HOWARD. I'm all aflutter.

ARTHUR. I've asked Lucille to marry me.

HOWARD. What?

ARTHUR. I've asked Lucille to marry me.

HOWARD. You have!

ARTHUR. Yes.

HOWARD. Well, that's great! Wow! You married! I don't even know what that means! Congratulations!

ARTHUR. She said yes.

HOWARD. Right. I didn't mean to jump the gun, but I assumed…. Who wouldn't marry you?!

ARTHUR. Lots of people.

HOWARD. You should've brought her to dinner! We could've …

ARTHUR. I wanted to talk to you first.

HOWARD. Oh. Okay.

ARTHUR. You know another reason you might've dreamed that I was the Fool is maybe just as simple as that. Maybe I am a fool, Howard. Maybe I know for a certainty I am a fool. A very big fool.

HOWARD. What are you talking about? What's the matter, Arthur?

ARTHUR. So I wanted to ask you, will you be my best man?

HOWARD. Oh, oh.

ARTHUR. I mean, if we are friends. And I don't really know if we are. I mean we've known each other for a long time …

HOWARD. Since that ghastly pub across from the Tate.

ARTHUR. I was so drunk.

11

HOWARD. You were hilarious.

ARTHUR. I don't really make friends with men.

HOWARD. Neither do I.

ARTHUR. We've talked a lot, but we don't know each other very well.

HOWARD. We know each other a tad bit more than a little.

ARTHUR. When you quit your job, changed your whole life, I had no idea that was coming. How well could I really know you and I didn't even have a suspicion such a big thing in your life was about to happen?

HOWARD. I didn't really know it myself.

ARTHUR. That I can understand. Sometimes a person can get so caught up in living their life, they can't see what's coming. But other people sometimes can. At least sensitive friends should be able to notice. But I don't know if that's what I am! I'm too subjective. I'm trapped in here, looking out through this slot.

HOWARD. Arthur. Arthur. I'd be delighted to be your best man.

ARTHUR. You would?

HOWARD. Of course I would, Arthur.

ARTHUR. You're sure?

HOWARD. I'm absolutely sure.

ARTHUR. That's great. That's great.

HOWARD. So you're going to marry Lucille.

ARTHUR. Yeah. That's the plan. In ten days.

HOWARD. In ten days! Wow! Quick.

ARTHUR. I've been waiting my whole life.

HOWARD. Arthur, you're a wild man!

ARTHUR. Lucille loves the idea. It's still a secret 'til she tells her parents.

HOWARD. Won't say a word. You and Lucille. Husband and wife.

ARTHUR. Yeah. That's the plan.

HOWARD. She's a beauty.

ARTHUR. Yeah. She's a looker.

HOWARD. She's like the sun coming up in the morning. She's like … Mexico!

ARTHUR.   Yeah, she's like Schliemann's Agamemnon mask.

HOWARD.   That's a bit esoteric. I mean, I don't know if you want to hear my impression of Lucille, but ...

ARTHUR.   Sure.

HOWARD.   She's got a gargantuan energy. She's like a hillbilly Aztec Evita.

ARTHUR.   I know. She's got scale!

HOWARD.   Alaska! I mean, she's an American girl!

ARTHUR.   Times Square!

HOWARD.   She's like Texas or something.

ARTHUR.   Well, she's from Texas.

HOWARD.   Right, well, that might go a long way toward explaining it. Her father is certainly a force of nature.

ARTHUR.   I know. I met him. Yosemite Sam in a Versace suit.

HOWARD.   Good customer. Formidable little fella. And you know, what you were saying before? My life suddenly took a big left hand turn and you hadn't even expected it was in the works? Well, we're even, because I didn't even have a clue that you were about to be married! And to Lucille.

ARTHUR.   Well, I'm secretive. So you'll be my best man?

HOWARD.   Absolutely!

ARTHUR.   Well, that's great. I do appreciate it.

HOWARD.   What's the matter?

ARTHUR.   We all have our secrets.

HOWARD.   Something on your mind?

ARTHUR.   Yes.

HOWARD.   Let me freshen that.

ARTHUR.   No, thank you. Howard. This is hard for me. I really need a friend right now. It's funny, I'm painting, I don't need a friend. I don't know the depth of our friendship. If Fate hadn't ... asserted my acting, I would never want to know.

HOWARD.   What is it?

ARTHUR.   It occurred to me.... Are you still reading psychiatric books?

HOWARD.   That's all I've been doing ... since we got back from the cruise. It's getting to be two years.

ARTHUR.   What got you up to read all those books? I mean, why didn't you get to a psychiatrist?

HOWARD. I didn't like the idea of it. I didn't like the idea of paying somebody. I'd had enough financial transactions, I guess. And I didn't want to come up against just one point of view. And I wanted to, you know, read the really big guys like Freud and Reich and Jung. I wanted to come up against them directly, feel their personalities. And also, I'm not the most trusting person. After what I've seen of human nature why would I be. I was at a very important moment in my life. I didn't want to entrust my soul to a stranger.

ARTHUR. You're smart.

HOWARD. That's not smart. That's a shortcoming.

ARTHUR. I've been going to a psychiatrist.

HOWARD. You have? When did you start?

ARTHUR. I've been going to a psychiatrist for six years.

HOWARD. Six years! You've been going to a psychiatrist for six years and you never mentioned it?!

ARTHUR. I told you, Howard. I'm secretive. I wouldn't have told you now if I could see a way around it.

HOWARD. But all this time when I've been talking about my ideas about the psyche and psychology, you've acted like it was all news to you!

ARTHUR. I was interested in what you had to say.

HOWARD. But you must've thought so much more than you said!

ARTHUR. Perhaps.

HOWARD. I mean, you were in the midst of having the experience of therapy!

ARTHUR. Yes, I was.

HOWARD. I would've been so interested in what you thought of my ideas in the light of your experience!

ARTHUR. I'm sorry.

HOWARD. It's all right. I'm sure you had your reasons.

ARTHUR. I did.

HOWARD. Boy, it's hard to know anybody.

ARTHUR. Have you ever thought of becoming an analyst yourself?

HOWARD. Me? Never! Doesn't interest me.

ARTHUR. Why not?

HOWARD. It's too toxic. All those unhealthy personalities, all that unhappiness. Those guys should wear protective clothing.

ARTHUR. True.

HOWARD. Think I'd be any good at it?

ARTHUR. I think you'd be good at anything you put your hand to. That's why I'm broaching this topic with you.

HOWARD. What topic?

ARTHUR. I want you to see my psychiatrist for me.

HOWARD. Come again?

ARTHUR. I want you to go to my psychiatrist.

HOWARD. You think I'm in trouble?

ARTHUR. No. Not you. Me. I know that I'm in trouble. This is very, very difficult for me.

HOWARD. Well, goddamnit, Arthur, you're gonna have to start talking a little more plainly!

ARTHUR. I know.

HOWARD. So?

ARTHUR. I have a problem.

HOWARD. You have a problem.

ARTHUR. I have a sexual problem.

HOWARD. You have a suh … sexual problem.

ARTHUR. Yes.

HOWARD. So you want me to go to a psychiatrist.

ARTHUR. Yes. My psychiatrist.

HOWARD. What's your sexual problem?

ARTHUR. I'm a fetishist.

HOWARD. I see. You're a fuh…. What kind of fetishist? *(No answer.)* What's your fetish?

ARTHUR. Socks.

HOWARD. Socks? Hose?

ARTHUR. You know, foot socks. Socks on the feet.

HOWARD. So. So let me backtrack. You're getting married to Lucille?

ARTHUR. Right.

HOWARD. You want me to stand up for you?

ARTHUR. Yes.

HOWARD. You're a fetishist?

ARTHUR. Yes. Socks.

HOWARD. Socks on the feet. And you want me to go to your psychiatrist?

ARTHUR. Yeah.

HOWARD. All right, go on.

ARTHUR. Well, my psychiatrist is a strict Freudian.

HOWARD. A Freudian. Jesus, my God, I mean well, if I'm anything, I'm a Jungian, but ... Arthur. Socks?

ARTHUR. I can't make love without these socks!

HOWARD. What?

ARTHUR. I can't make love without these socks!

HOWARD. What socks? You mean there's some specific socks?

ARTHUR. My father's socks.

HOWARD. You can't make love without your father's socks?

ARTHUR. But with the socks, I'm fine! I have no problem at all! I just need the socks.

HOWARD. I'm speechless.

ARTHUR. I just need the socks.

HOWARD. Does Lucille know about this?

ARTHUR. No.

HOWARD. Yow.

ARTHUR. I don't have to have them on. It's not like I have to have them on.

HOWARD. No?

ARTHUR. I just have to know where they are. Be able to touch them. At the crucial moment.

HOWARD. Ah shit!

ARTHUR. This is hard.

HOWARD. I feel ashamed.

ARTHUR. You? How do you think I feel?

HOWARD. You.... How can I put this! You risk so much in telling me this.

ARTHUR. I have no choice.

HOWARD. You know what this is? This is intimacy.

ARTHUR. I guess so.

HOWARD. No! This is real intimacy. Now it's my turn.

ARTHUR. What?

HOWARD. A year ago, I tried to get my job back.

ARTHUR. Are we talking about you?

16

HOWARD. They didn't want me.

ARTHUR. But I thought …

HOWARD. That's what I wanted you to think. That it was all my choice. It was at first. Then I changed my mind. And I found out they were glad I was gone. They like the new guy. Jerry. He's cheaper than I was and does just as well. Maybe better.

ARTHUR. Why didn't you tell me?

HOWARD. I was humiliated. I didn't want anyone to know. I'm very proud.

ARTHUR. Nothing wrong with pride.

HOWARD. Yes, there is. I didn't even have the courage to go to therapy.

ARTHUR. No, with you it was a choice.

HOWARD. Oh. I put the best face on everything!

ARTHUR. But you've done a good job on yourself, read all those books. Figured out your …

HOWARD. I helped myself, yes. But that just fed my pride, and it's my pride that's gotten entrenched. I still don't know what to do with the rest of my life, and I'm never able to let that question alone. I have this energy in me like a tiger and it tears at me. I don't know what to do with it. You telling me this incredibly personal sexual detail, it makes me ashamed of how I've been unwilling to show you my weakness.

ARTHUR. That's all right.

HOWARD. No. it's not all right! I just wanted to posture at being superior to you! I'm Lear and you're the Fool. It's insulting! I'm setting myself up as a King and calling you names while I'm at it! I'm the one who should be in therapy all this time, not you! You're a good man. A good man and no more than a man, but then you don't pretend to be!

ARTHUR. Therapy's not so great. I've been going for six years, and I still need the socks.

HOWARD. So how did you ascertain you were ready for marriage?

ARTHUR. I made a decision. I accepted my shortcomings.

HOWARD. Were you going to tell Lucille?

ARTHUR. No. I accepted them privately.

HOWARD. What does your psychiatrist think?

ARTHUR. Dr. Block still thinks I can be cured.

HOWARD. But you don't think so?

ARTHUR. No.

HOWARD. And this Dr. Block, is he good?

ARTHUR. He's more than competent.

HOWARD. He's the psychiatrist you want me to see?

ARTHUR. I'd really appreciate it.

HOWARD. Why?

ARTHUR. Well, this may sound strange and maybe paranoid. I'm worried that my psychiatrist may be … evil.

HOWARD. You don't mean 'evil?'

ARTHUR. Yes. It could be something else. He says it's something else, but I don't really believe him.

HOWARD. What do you base this on?

ARTHUR. Well. He's taken my socks.

HOWARD. What?

ARTHUR. He's taken my socks and he won't give them back.

HOWARD. Why not?

ARTHUR. He asked to…. You know I'd been talking about them, and he asked to see them, and now he's got them and he won't give them back.

HOWARD. You're kidding.

ARTHUR. No, I'm not kidding. Now I'm supposed to be getting married and I need those socks. I didn't know who to talk to about this. I don't want Lucille to know. I can't really go to the police. I really wouldn't want to explain this to the police.

HOWARD. You've confronted him yourself?

ARTHUR. He threatened to destroy them.

HOWARD. No.

ARTHUR. He had a cigarette lighter. I became hysterical and backed off. Howard, I asked you to be my best man because you're the only man I know I consider may be a friend. I wanted to enlist you in the cause of my marriage. You're a driven man, I know that. So is this Dr. Block. If I go to some psychiatric association or something, I can't help but think their bias is going to favor one of their own over a pathetic fetishist who wants his socks back.

HOWARD.   But they'd have to understand this guy's in the wrong.

ARTHUR.   He's very clever! What I need is someone to go in there, under the guise of being a patient, take this guy's measure, maybe get the socks. I need you.

HOWARD.   I don't know ...

ARTHUR.   What are you going to do, read those books 'til you go blind? Or are you going to apply what you've learned to save a man's life? My life. I'm in jeopardy! Listen, Howard, if this engagement goes bust, I'll fall to pieces. There won't be enough glue in the world. I have nothing to induce you. Friendship. Lucille said she'd marry me. I hold that like a golden lantern in a dark world. If that lantern goes out, and it will go out if I don't get those socks back, it all goes dark for me. You're my last hope, my best man. Say you'll do it. I'm a beggar! Please! Please!

HOWARD.   All right I will.

ARTHUR.   You will?

HOWARD.   Yes, I'll do it. I'll go. And guess what? I'll get the socks.

ARTHUR.   Do you think you could?

HOWARD.   Arthur, you can take it to the bank.

ARTHUR.   God bless you, Howard.

HOWARD.   Say no more about it. His name is Dr. Block?

ARTHUR.   Yes. He's got my future like a hostage.

HOWARD.   He's a Freudian.

ARTHUR.   Yes.

HOWARD.   Why did you go to a Freudian?

ARTHUR.   I don't know. I was in a hurry.

HOWARD.   No, everything's for a reason. I've been sitting here reading these books the human mind for two years. I didn't realize it, but I've been preparing for something. Sharpening my sword for a confrontation. Dr. Block.

ARTHUR.   I think he may really be evil.

HOWARD.   We'll see. We'll see.

FADE TO BLACK

Scene 2

Dr. Block's office. The leather wing chair appears again, now with an Oriental throw pillow. In this chair sits Dr. Block. He's a powerful man with a Bronx accent. There's the classic couch for therapy. Howard stands initially. Both men are edgy, like wrestlers looking for an advantage.

BLOCK. So how do you care to be addressed?

HOWARD. Howard.

BLOCK. They call me Dr. Block.

HOWARD. You're not German.

BLOCK. Am I supposed to be German?

HOWARD. I associate Freudian psychiatry with Germans.

BLOCK. You seem more sophisticated than that assumption suggests, Howard.

HOWARD. Perhaps I'm not.

BLOCK. I was born and raised in the Bronx. My father was in fact German, my mother English, and I guess I'm very much the American. We'll start with your childhood.

HOWARD. No we won't. *(Pause.)*

BLOCK. All right, where do you want to start?

HOWARD. What do you think of Jung's split with Freud?

BLOCK. Oh Christ crucified! Your unconscious is completely contaminated by some half-baked exposure to psychoanalytic literature! Isn't it?

HOWARD. No.

BLOCK. You've read things?

HOWARD. Yes.

BLOCK. I hate that in a patient! I can see you're testing me.

HOWARD. That's true.

BLOCK. I intuit that you'd like to know if I'm intuitive because that would demonstrate sensitivity, a trait that you hold very highly. Correct?

HOWARD. Correct.

BLOCK. All right, I can do that for you. To a point. You're a power devil. Before you could trust me, you'd have to pass a

20

piece of emotional legislation longer than the Magna Carta. You think you know better. You're insular. Probably have a wife like an orbiting satellite. If you don't discover it for yourself, a concept doesn't exist. If it's forced on you that someone else does have an insight or construct that goes beyond the borders of your ruminations and yet has validity, you have to choke back garbage cans of rage. Most likely you'll avoid such people and then wonder aloud where they are?! Where are your peers? You exist in lonely splendor. But! But! Something's gone wrong. In the words of your precious Carl Jung, enantiadromia's set in. That is, the reversal of a man's fortune. Always a horrible dilemma and spiritual crisis for a man who's held sway over a small, self-created kingdom. Why are the plants dying in my precious terrarium? The confident corner of your mouth sags under the weight of new, unwanted knowledge. You don't even believe you're here for yourself. You had to fool yourself into it somehow. That it was for someone else's good. Your wife? No, it would have to be a man. Because that's who you're in competition with. The race of men. That's the reverse side of the coin. Tails. The tales you tell yourself. But the obverse side of the coin is your longing for the love of a man. True love! So unattainable! The bluebird you chase in your private dreams. A true friend. A man you could talk to. Now all is in ruins. The side of yourself that longed for a male confidant is still inexpressibly disappointed by your experience of friendship. Why? Because you will not choose a peer and lose your precious superiority! And the bold dragon slayer in you that succeeded so in the world has become the prisoner of his own armor. Trapped in his rusting jail in the rain, while others, lesser men all, divide the loot that is rightly his. Have I named you, Howard?

HOWARD. I don't agree with all of that!

BLOCK. Well, my God man, why would you?! That would be a terrible admission indeed. The man I've described is little more than a giant bleeding ego in a vacuum of his own creation. Tell me one of your dreams. Come on! I've risked a lot showing you the depth of what I see. I deserve your candor.

HOWARD. I'm not ready to do that.

BLOCK. Better. All right. Something easier. Tell me your recent history.

HOWARD. All right. I managed a large and extremely successful mutual fund …

BLOCK. But not anymore.

HOWARD. I quit two years ago.

BLOCK. Why?

HOWARD. I felt like I was missing the experience of life.

BLOCK. I'm sure you were. Who replaced you?

HOWARD. Why do you ask that? Someone named Jerry something.

BLOCK. Oh, we don't like him, do we? You can't remember his last name?

HOWARD. No.

BLOCK. Then your emotions went haywire.

HOWARD. Yes.

BLOCK. Did you try to get your job back?

HOWARD. Yes.

BLOCK. And you couldn't get it back.

HOWARD. No.

BLOCK. That must've been a jolt.

HOWARD. Yes.

BLOCK. Now look, Howard, if you feel awful and you want to feel better, tell me a dream.

HOWARD. All right. *(He lays down on the couch.)* I dreamed I was a Roman, and I was supposed to commit suicide. With a dagger. And my suicide was being overseen by a Greek. I was very emotional, kneeling, calling out to God to give me the courage to stab myself. The Greek looked on coolly.

BLOCK. Now I know, because you're a complete power devil, that you told me a dream that you already feel you've analyzed very well. So tell me your interpretation.

HOWARD. Well, I feel it's a dream about my personality being out of balance. I think my Roman side, the business side of myself, the road builder if you will, has been overused in my job …

BLOCK. I see. And the Greek side, your artistic, non-linear side, was stepping in and demanding equal time.

HOWARD.   Something like that. *(Block laughs.)* What's funny?

BLOCK.   I'm sorry. Forgive me. It's just that sometimes the relentlessly self-serving analysis of the eager amateur tickles me in my aching bones. God, I bet you've read a lot of books!

HOWARD.   Yes. I have. Is that a bad thing?

BLOCK.   Yes, it is! Mostly by Carl Gustav Jung I imagine.

HOWARD.   As it happens.

BLOCK.   You know. Carl Jung's ghost came to me one night. Came to my bedroom and woke me out of a profound slumber.

HOWARD.   Are you serious?

BLOCK.   Yes I'm serious.

HOWARD.   But I thought you were a Freudian?

BLOCK.   I'm a man, Howard. Utterly different from you. And I've had many experiences. Of which you know nothing. This dream is a homosexual revenge fantasy.

HOWARD.   *(Jumps off the couch.)* What!

BLOCK.   The Roman whom you identify as you is in fact the man who replaced you. Jerry. He is the one who has usurped your Roman identity and towards whom you bear a murderous rage. The Greek, who we know historically was subjugated by the Roman, is seen here in the dominant position. What else are the Greeks known for?

HOWARD.   Their art.

BLOCK.   Come on! Christ crucified! In my neighborhood they used to say, if you drop something, don't bend over to get it if a Greek is around.

HOWARD.   That's just ignorance.

BLOCK.   The Greek is standing, *(He kneels before Howard.)* the Roman is on his knees, holding a dagger before him. If I looked at this picture without my glasses on, what do you think I'd see?

HOWARD.   But I was the Roman!

BLOCK.   'Til you were replaced by Jerry.

HOWARD.   But I was the Roman in the dream!

BLOCK.   Come on, work for me a little. What is Jerry's last name?

HOWARD.   I know it's weird, but I can never seem to re-

23

member.

BLOCK.   And yet you must know. Have you spoken to him since then?

HOWARD.   Oh yes, he calls me fairly often.

BLOCK.   Why?

HOWARD.   For advice. On the management of the portfolio.

BLOCK.   And do you give him good advice?

HOWARD.   Moderately …

BLOCK.   What's Jerry's last name?

HOWARD.   Pulaski. No. Polansky. That's it.

BLOCK.   Jerry Polansky.

HOWARD.   Yeah, that's his name. Well, that's a relief.

BLOCK.   Does it ring a bell? Polansky?

HOWARD.   No.

BLOCK.   Can you think of anyone else you know by that name?

HOWARD.   No.

BLOCK.   Have you ever heard of anyone else by that name?

HOWARD.   No. Well. Roman Polanski … but —

BLOCK.   Roman. Polanski.

HOWARD.   Roman Polanski.

BLOCK.   So you see your dream is not a noble struggle toward balance and artistry. It is a dream in which Jerry the Roman Polanski is on his knees before you, where you supervise and participate in his sexual humiliation for the purpose of destroying him. Your rival. The man who bested you.

HOWARD.   I know that's not what that dream's about!

BLOCK.   They drove Roman Polanski out of the country! Would that satisfy you?!

HOWARD.   Yes! No!

BLOCK.   Do you feel angry?

HOWARD.   Yes!

BLOCK.   Good. I'm glad you know how you feel. If that's not what the dream's about, why couldn't you remember his last name?

HOWARD.   I don't know!

BLOCK.   It's the key to the dream. You repressed the name because it was a clue. A clue that identified the Roman in the dream not as you, but as Jerry. And if Jerry is the Roman in your dream, and his murder's being supervised, then who shall we suppose is the supervisor? But you. Revealed not to be a saint, or wise old Aristotle, but a mean-spirited little rat. Fantasizing revenge. To sum up. Listen closely. The dream is a sexually based wish fulfillment.

HOWARD. You've attacked my pride, which I feel needs to be attacked, so I'm reluctant to defend myself.

BLOCK. How noble of you! And yet we know from your dream that your true face is not so kingly.

HOWARD. I admit that your interpretation ...

BLOCK. Don't waste my time and this session aping the demeanor of a generous man. It's laughable and boring. So I gather that you're feeding this Jerry character bad advice hoping that he'll fall on his face? You're not really helping him with these phone calls, am I right?

HOWARD. I withhold the best of my analysis.

BLOCK. But your tone, I'm sure, is very helpful.

HOWARD. Yes.

BLOCK. You pretend to be rooting for this.... What do you think of him as? A jerk?

HOWARD. I just think he's not as sophisticated as I am.

BLOCK. Well, who could be? He's a jerk! He's a moron! You wish he was dead! You'd like to kick him in the throat and watch him choke! Wouldn't you? WOULDN'T YOU?!

HOWARD. I wouldn't go as far as that.

BLOCK. Oh yes you would, Howard, rhymes with Coward, if you thought nobody would know. Wouldn't you love to open the paper and see Jerry's dead body there? Stabbed to death in a cheap motel by a male hustler let's say?

HOWARD. What're you ... if you ...

BLOCK. Did you catch that story in the paper by the way? I mean that happened a while ago?

HOWARD. What?

BLOCK. The male hustler upright businessman cheap motel scenario did play out for some unlucky somebody.

HOWARD. I think I did see something about it.

BLOCK. Before or after your dream?

HOWARD. GO TO HELL!

BLOCK. And I'd watch that over-innocent, foolish Jerry if I were you. Those advice-soliciting phone calls of his. Sounds to me like he's a bit of a sadist giving you a bit of the knife.

HOWARD. What do you mean?

BLOCK. Your bad advice doesn't seem to be losing him his job.

HOWARD. He doesn't always take it.

BLOCK. Well, that must smart.

HOWARD. It's to be expected.

BLOCK. Sounds to me like he's your cat and you're his birdy lunch.

HOWARD. Maybe there's a bit of that about the calls.

BLOCK. So now who referred you to me? *(Looks at note pad.)* Oh. Arthur. Arthur. Well, that makes sense.

HOWARD. He's getting married.

BLOCK. So he says.

HOWARD. He's asked me to be the best man.

BLOCK. And you agreed of course.

HOWARD. I agreed.

BLOCK. Even though you're not close enough, truly close enough, to be his best man. But you agreed because you're so hungry for an outward show of qualities that you do not, in fact, possess.

HOWARD. Such as?

BLOCK. Can you hear yourself? Your hollow tone of, what, invulnerability.

HOWARD. I can hear myself. So what qualities do I not, in fact, possess? Such as?

BLOCK. Being a good friend. So I began to tell you how Carl Jung's ghost came to my room. For several months, I had been reading and rereading and reading Jung. I kept feeling that I was getting close, frustratingly close, to understanding the man. But something was missing. A mystery at the core of his being. He kept referring to his experience of the numinous, the holy, but he would never allow me to have that experience. It was an erroneous longing on my part in the sense that, well, get your own! I needed to have my own experience of the Godhead or the living universe, but I wanted Jung's. In a way, he created that desire in me, the way a rock star creates an unquenchable fervor in the breast of his groupie. Jung was a seductor. To be fair, as was Freud. They let you glimpse something golden and wonderful, but there was no way to acquire it for yourself. Neither stuck to the *Ding Han Sich,* the thing in itself. Look. I'm speaking German! I'm getting more Freudian for you!

HOWARD.   Thank you. Are you a seductor?

BLOCK.   Quite the contrary. So I'd been reading Jung to the point of saturation, and thrilled by the direction of his mind. Frustrated but thrilled. And I went to bed one night, and I had this dream. I dreamed that Carl Jung and I were supposed to get on this train. And we got on this train. And just as it was leaving, I stepped off. And Jung went choo-choo, away. And then I woke up. I was in a hypnogogic state, that is a state of hypnosis induced by sleep, in which the eyes are open, and the unconscious sees. And I could feel Jung's ghost in the room. Like a heavy, Teutonic uncle. I could feel him. I could feel his presence. And I didn't like it!

HOWARD.   Why?

BLOCK.   He felt evil. He felt evil to me.

HOWARD.   Is this therapy?!

BLOCK.   Jung described therapy as the interaction of a healthy and an unhealthy spirit.

HOWARD.   Which one are you?

BLOCK.   Arthur has a problem. Are you aware of his problem?

HOWARD.   My God. Dr. Block, you're not about to betray Arthur's confidence?! You are a professional, aren't you?!

BLOCK.   So you do know.

HOWARD.   Yes.

BLOCK.   So of course then it's Arthur. Arthur is the excuse you're using to seek out help for yourself.

HOWARD.   You think that Jung might be evil. Arthur thinks that you might be evil.

BLOCK.   I have no doubt. Tell me another dream.

HOWARD.   Are you?

BLOCK.   I'll leave that for you to decide. Tell me another

dream.

HOWARD.   I dreamed that I was King Lear and that Arthur was The Fool. That's all I remember.

BLOCK.   *Your* Fool. But you do see how you're up to your old tricks.

HOWARD.   What do you mean?

BLOCK.   You switched.

HOWARD.   What?

BLOCK.   You've switched them again, the characters in your dream. To avoid understanding. Arthur's the King, not you. You're the Fool. His Fool. One man's fool is another man's stockbroker.

HOWARD.   No, I was Arthur, I mean, I was Lear. In the dream.

BLOCK.   I believe they call that a Freudian slip. So how long have we been at this and we have a wish fulfillment of a sexual nature and a Freudian slip. Are you sure you don't want to start with your childhood, Howard? Never mind. Yes. You are The Fool and Arthur, as we all know, is the King. King Arthur. It's always King Arthur, it's never King Howard. In your relationship with Arthur, it's you perhaps who see the more clearly, but it's Arthur who has the power. It's Arthur who rules. The monarch.

HOWARD.   But that's not our relationship.

BLOCK.   No? You think you have the upper hand? Well, of course you believe you have the upper hand. Otherwise, you wouldn't be friends with Arthur. It would be too threatening. But is that the reality? It was Arthur who asked you to come to see me, right?

HOWARD.   Yes.

BLOCK.   And you're here. Has your wife ever suggested that you see a psychiatrist?

HOWARD.   Yes.

BLOCK.   Did you go?

HOWARD.   No. I wanted to cure myself.

BLOCK.   Egomaniac. *(Pause.)* But when Arthur asked you to see a psychiatrist, you came.

HOWARD.   He was asking me as a favor! He was in trouble!

BLOCK.   You're in trouble!

HOWARD. You violate everything I understand to be the therapeutic process, Dr. Block!

BLOCK. Of course I do, Howard! I'm a quack! I'm a crackpot!

HOWARD. You admit it?

BLOCK. I'm the only one who can help you, and I don't know if I care to!

HOWARD. I'm not here for your help!

BLOCK. Oh, I forgot! You're above it all! You understand the value of submitting to therapy *for others,* but you can take care of yourself!

HOWARD. If I did want psychiatric help, I would go to somebody reputable!

BLOCK. But that's obviously untrue! You have gone to someone, ME, and I'm a quack!

HOWARD. You're actually calling yourself a quack?

BLOCK. I stole Arthur's socks!

HOWARD. You admit it?

BLOCK. Yes! I stole his precious socks! I must be a quack! And you, obviously, are on the side of the angels. Arthur's wedding night approaches, his bride-to-be is in the dark about his problem ...

HOWARD. That's none of your business!

BLOCK. And you, ever anxious to prove that you have a heart, that you are a friend, and that you're not impotent *in the world,* are here to save the day! Well, save it!

HOWARD. Is there something I'm missing?

BLOCK. There's a lot you're missing. As you've already admitted. The experience of life itself.

HOWARD. Oh. Oh. I don't know. I feel disturbed. *(Block opens a drawer and takes out an old pair of argyle socks.)*

BLOCK. Here. Boom. Nothing. The socks. *(Howard doesn't take them.)*

HOWARD. You'd give them back?

BLOCK. Yes.

HOWARD. Just like that?

BLOCK. Just like that.

HOWARD. I won't deny that the things you've said about me

contain some elements of truth ...

BLOCK. I don't care what you'll admit or deny. I have no respect for you. I have no interest in you. Take the socks and go.

HOWARD. How did you get your low opinion?

BLOCK. You came into my office under false pretenses. You have a man you call a *friend.* He has a severe neurotic symptom. You enjoy an unequal relationship with this man. He appeals to your vanity and you rise to the bait like a self-satisfied, soon-to-be-fried catfish! You want to give a man a crutch so he'll limp forever. I want to kick the crutch away and exhort him to walk! Who is this man's friend? Who is this man's enemy? Do you want the socks or not? *(Howard doesn't reach for them. Block continues to offer. Howard begins to cry.)*

HOWARD. No. No. Take them away.

BLOCK. Your reasons are still too disgusting! Now you want my approval! It's all about you! You just want to be the best man! You don't give a damn about the bride and groom!

HOWARD. I don't know how you've done it, but you've made me feel very ashamed.

BLOCK. The shame was there. *(He lowers the socks.)* You've done things for which you should feel shame. And like all people who do mischief, you prefer to do it in the dark. Where mirrors do not function. Where you're not forced to see the ugliness of your deeds. *(Block puts the socks away.)*

HOWARD. I'm sorry.

BLOCK. Are you?

HOWARD. I am sorry.

BLOCK. Don't tell me. Tell Arthur. *(Strikes a gavel.)* End of session!

BLACKOUT

ACT TWO

Scene 1

The sitting room of a Park Avenue apartment done up Texas style. High Texas style, on the order of Giant. *There's a gold-framed picture of young John Wayne. Lucille, a big beautiful blond in her late twenties, is on the phone. She's in a fabulous wedding dress. She's eating a banana.*

LUCILLE. Sunflowers! Sunflowers, that will be my bouquet! I will not be contradicted! Daddy, he's not a deadbeat, he's an artist! No, that does not mean vagrant. I don't know if he's any good! I don't know about such things. But he is going to be my husband. That's what you have to deal with. What's Mommy say? Well, you listen to her. I'm wearing it now. It's not bad luck for me to see it! What's she saying? Put her on. Mommy, how do you keep him off the furniture? White. It's white. Pure white. Well, what was I gonna do? Put the approximate number of dots on it? I don't know what you'd call the style other than just classic. It's a beautiful dress. Well, I couldn't very well do that, could I? Your dress is forty years old. It's yellow. It's yellow like an old man's teeth is yellow! *(Knocking comes at the door.)* I'm coming, Ellie! *(To phone.)* It's Ellie. I gotta go. YOU take care! Get that old crank to take you to the Crescent Court for lunch! Make him buy you a Bloody Mary. You tell him I said! I'll be back on with you tonight. *(A sweet doorbell rings. Lucille opens the door. Ellie is standing there in a blue dress.)* Ellie!
ELLIE. Lucille!
LUCILLE. Oh, my people are driving me nuts!
ELLIE. Look at you.
LUCILLE. I mean, they're happy. Wedding bells. But it's all higgledy piggledy quick.
ELLIE. I know. Can we talk about what you're wearing? Is this ...
LUCILLE. Tra-la-la-la-la.
ELLIE. My God! You're in your wedding dress.
LUCILLE. Do I look like a big napkin?

ELLIE. Is this the actual dress?

LUCILLE. This is the very dress. Maybe. If I continue to like it. What do you think?

ELLIE. It's fabulous. It's a fabulous dress.

LUCILLE. The dressmaker tacked it together for me so I could, you know, make war with myself over it. Do you really think that it's.... Do I look like a fool?

ELLIE. No. You look like a gift. A wonderful gift.

LUCILLE. I was going to go to this place on Madison. Mommy asked her friends in Dallas and they said that this Tommy King's on Madison was *the* place for a wedding dress. So I made an appointment and went to Tommy King's. Sit down, you look pale. I show up to the sound of gunfire!

ELLIE. Oh God. This was on the radio!

LUCILLE. Two local pistoleros held the place up!

ELLIE. Wasn't a man shot?

LUCILLE. Yes. Want some tea? I have some tea here.

ELLIE. Sure.

LUCILLE. They shot a bridegroom in the armpit and took a woman in a wedding dress as a hostage! I'm standing.... I can't remember this minute, you take sugar?

ELLIE. I will today.

LUCILLE. I'm standing on Madison Avenue. Gunshot. Window busts out. I see this maniac holding a thirty-two under the chin of this bride he's dragging into the street.

ELLIE. I don't know how much longer I can live in New York.

LUCILLE. Dallas isn't any better. They mugged my mother in a parking lot and she knows karate. Anyway, I looked at that hostage and I don't care what they say. I did NOT like the dress.

ELLIE. You're too much.

LUCILLE. So I found out about this dressmaker, she came to me, and do you really think it's all right?

ELLIE. It's great. You look like a swan.

LUCILLE. I can't drink anymore of this. Tastes like shellac! I know it's wrong, but would you mind if I had a beer?

ELLIE. You're safe with me.

LUCILLE. You're a doll, baby.

ELLIE.   I love your makeup!

LUCILLE.   It's just base! *(She's gotten a beer.)*

ELLIE.   Then it's your face!

LUCILLE.   No, it's the base! It's just lots and lots of base! Later I'll sketch in some details.

ELLIE.   I can't believe you're going to give this place up. It's so you.

LUCILLE.   That's the urban dance we do. The guy who lived here before me was a painter. Like Arthur. This is northern light. He told me northern light is the best light.

ELLIE.   Why?

LUCILLE.   Because it's constant. You can depend on northern light. Other light is fickle.

ELLIE.   Well, I'm going to jump in. I bring news.

LUCILLE.   What kind of news?

ELLIE.   Howard is seeing a psychiatrist!

LUCILLE.   You mean, a head doctor? What for?

ELLIE.   Well, don't be parochial, Lucille. People do go to psychiatrists. It's not a stigma.

LUCILLE.   It's not a bonus.

ELLIE.   It's a common thing.

LUCILLE.   So's curvature of the spine. Come on, what does Howard need with that? He's home free.

ELLIE.   Well, it was Arthur. Arthur got him to go.

LUCILLE.   Arthur? My Arthur?

ELLIE.   Yes, your Arthur! Arthur got Howard to go to his psychiatrist.

LUCILLE.   Arthur goes to a psychiatrist?

ELLIE.   You didn't know that?

LUCILLE.   No.

ELLIE.   I was hoping you knew that.

LUCILLE.   Why would Arthur go to a psychiatrist?

ELLIE.   Why?

LUCILLE.   Why?

ELLIE.   Well, you know, for his problem.

LUCILLE.   Which problem is that?

ELLIE.   That he's a…. What's the word?

LUCILLE.   I don't have the word.

ELLIE.   That he's a fetishist.

LUCILLE.   What's that?

ELLIE.   You don't know what a fetishist is?

LUCILLE.   I guess I sort've do. But I didn't know I was about to marry one.

ELLIE.   Oh my God. I'm sorry, Lucille.

LUCILLE.   What's his fetish?

ELLIE.   Maybe you should talk to Arthur.

LUCILLE.   WHAT'S HIS FETISH, ELEANOR?

ELLIE.   Socks.

LUCILLE.   Thank you. I've known you the better part of eight years, Eleanor. I value our friendship. Socks.

ELLIE.   I thought you knew.

LUCILLE.   No, you didn't. But I suppose there's no graceful way into that one.

ELLIE.   No, there isn't. Listen, everybody has something wrong with them.

LUCILLE.   Socks.

ELLIE.   Yeah.

LUCILLE.   You know, Arthur and I, we've had experiences. I've never seen these socks.

ELLIE.   I know.

LUCILLE.   What do you mean, you know? Well, what else do you know? Am I blushing?! God damn it, I'm blushing!

ELLIE.   I …

LUCILLE.   I what? Yes I'm listening!

ELLIE.   Oh God, Lucille, I'm sorry! I might as well come at this straight! Howard told me this just awful stuff about Arthur! That he's a pervert! That he needs these socks to perform! That he's kept you completely in the dark! Through six years of desperate, dead-end therapy! He still needs these dirty little argyle socks secreted on or about his person or he cannot do the deed! You know I love you, Lucille! Despite my natural competitive ambivalence. You know I want good things for you! Howard and Arthur have been trying to handle this themselves, but we both know that when it comes to matters of the heart, or even more, matters of sex, men are cartoon characters.

LUCILLE.   Why did Howard tell you? Why didn't Arthur tell

me?

ELLIE.   Shame.

LUCILLE.   Shame indeed! And fear for his life! Oh God, look at me in this dress! I'm a travesty of myself! What am I going to tell my mother? What am I going to tell my father?! What am I going to do? I can't marry him now.

ELLIE.   I admit it looks problematic.

LUCILLE.   I can't marry him under these circumstances! The whole thing's purple!

ELLIE.   We might as well get it all out. The circumstances are worse than you know. Arthur's socks have been stolen and he is no longer a man!

LUCILLE.   Maybe I'll try the tea again.

ELLIE.   Arthur's psychiatrist is a nut. He took Arthur's magic creepy socks and he won't give them back. There. That's the news. And that's the problem. If this gets out ...

LUCILLE.   BUT IT'S NOT GOING TO GET OUT.

ELLIE.   Of course not.

LUCILLE.   Who knows?

ELLIE.   Me. The shrink. Howard.

LUCILLE.   Howard's afraid of you, right?

ELLIE.   And with good reason.

LUCILLE.   All right then, first of all. You tell Howard, if he speaks of this, he's dead.

ELLIE.   Okay. That's fair.

LUCILLE.   And as for you, Ellie. You know I love you.

ELLIE.   And I love you, Lucille.

LUCILLE.   I respect you. I've learned a lot from you. If you speak of this, even though it would break my heart, I will rip your throat out.

ELLIE.   Okay. That is also fair.

LUCILLE.   I know it's good gossip.

ELLIE.   The best I ever came across in my life.

LUCILLE.   But if you succumb to the temptation, I will drive you out of the universe.

ELLIE.   Okay. I understand.

LUCILLE.   I had to choose an artist.

ELLIE.   He's cute. He's straight. Sort've straight.

LUCILLE. He's about as straight as the number eight. How could I get taken in like this?

ELLIE. You really didn't know at all?

LUCILLE. We talk about what we read in the magazines, the ins and outs among our friends. Do I seem savvy or naive?

ELLIE. Savvy. Texas savvy. But very savvy.

LUCILLE. I always thought I was a good study. When it came to human nature. Who's in the photograph. Who sits with who. Who's a social climber. I can look at a woman's shoes and know if she's a hypocrite. I believe I can.

ELLIE. I know you can.

LUCILLE. Arthur doesn't know any of this stuff. Ellie, how did he take me in?

ELLIE. I don't know. Women get fooled.

LUCILLE. I feel like my cake just fell.

ELLIE. You're still the greatest.

LUCILLE. No, you pity me now. I'm one of those women with one of those men.

ELLIE. Oh, I can't stand to see you this way.

LUCILLE. I'm gonna be pathetic. I might as well move to Texarkana and become a Baptist.

ELLIE. Now come on, get a hold of yourself!

LUCILLE. That's easy for you to say, you've got Howard.

ELLIE. Well, yes I do.

LUCILLE. You're set up like a queen in her cake shop with her king on his throne.

ELLIE. I have my problems.

LUCILLE. Come on, you've told me about your life. It's good.

ELLIE. I have my problems. But problems can be solved. You have Arthur. I have Howard.

LUCILLE. So?

ELLIE. Do you recall that cruise Howard and I took?

LUCILLE. The cruise? The fabulous cruise?

ELLIE. Of course I told you it was fabulous, but no it was not fabulous.

LUCILLE. It wasn't.

ELLIE. No, it was horrible.

LUCILLE. But you told me ...

ELLIE.   Yes, I told you it was wonderful, BUT I WAS LYING. Isn't that the point? We all want to look good. As you just demonstrated, no woman worth knowing wants her significant man perceived as a calamity. I have to appear to have the winning hand or how can I socialize. But you can't build a life on just appearance. Howard had a nervous breakdown.
LUCILLE.   He did not!
ELLIE.   Lucille, like a house of cards. He started raving, writing these crazy notes, breaking down sobbing on the Stairmaster. I mean, three months of ... hell.
LUCILLE.   You mean both our men are crazy?!
ELLIE.   No. I mean both our men are MEN. This fetish thing is not the worst thing and it's not going to be the last thing. Men unravel ever further. Howard's histrionics on the high seas were just the first stop on a downward spiral. Howard found these psychological books and started talking this mythical stuff and just everything was a myth! He went to the dentist, it was a myth. Two guys started a deli, they were Romulus and Remus. He consulted the cabala. He read a passage from the Book of Genesis at our co-op meeting. Howard went to his company, tried to get his job back. No soap. That night he called Psychic Hotline and tried to find the Future I guess. Ran up quite a bill. MEANWHILE. We were the first ten steps down the road to destitution.
LUCILLE.   So. You're broke and I'm a fool.
ELLIE.   I'm not broke.
LUCILLE.   You've got private money?
ELLIE.   I've got potash.
LUCILLE.   Pot what?
ELLIE.   Potash. I had a problem. I found a solution. Potash. It's a natural resource. A fertilizer for fruit. You can invest in it. I did. I invested in some other things as well. Howard reads his books, and I took over the management of our assets. Turns out I have a knack for commodities.
LUCILLE.   Here all this time I thought Howard was supporting you.
ELLIE.   We'd be in the street. *(Looks at the Wayne portrait.)* John Wayne.

LUCILLE.   Did you think about leaving him?

ELLIE.   Howard? Never! Yes. But I decided that I would be just as wrong about the next man I married, so I might as well continue down my own boulevard of surprises. I think we're in the middle of finding a kind of happiness. And you can find happiness, too, Lucille. That's what I'm telling you. That's my point. You can forge happiness with almost anybody. It's just a long-term kind of excavating pet project. Did you hang this picture of John Wayne?

LUCILLE.   Would a decorator do that? Of course I hung it. Ellie, what am I gonna do?

ELLIE.   You have a problem. There is a solution. You're gonna marry Arthur.

LUCILLE.   I can't marry Arthur now!

ELLIE.   Yes, you can!

LUCILLE.   Oh, the whole thing's tainted now! What's the point of a wedding if it's not perfect? Here's my father against Arthur anyway, and how am I gonna look him in the eye with conviction and say Nay?! My mother's just gonna eat lemons over this! I have a sister in Michigan who'll be pleased. Damn it! Damn it! I want a big, strong, confident, take-charge man!

ELLIE.   You want John Wayne.

LUCILLE.   I don't know. I'd take John Wayne, I'll tell you that.

ELLIE.   But you didn't choose John Wayne. You chose Arthur. You chose an obscure, penniless painter who's kind of difficult to read.

LUCILLE.   He conned me into thinking he was somebody else!

ELLIE.   But the point you made before was true, Lucille. You're not naive. You're savvy.

LUCILLE.   Oh, don't repeat me back to me.

ELLIE.   You must've known what he was.

LUCILLE.   Did you know what Howard was?

ELLIE.   I still don't know what Howard is. I only know the dance we do. But I chose him! I certainly did! And you chose Arthur!

LUCILLE.   But why?! Why would I do a thing like that?! I'm not one of these New York girls. I like to be happy! *(As if she*

38

heard somebody say it.) And I'm not my mother, either!

ELLIE.   I didn't say you were.

LUCILLE.   Well, forget it 'cause I'm not! I'm nothing like her. And Arthur is nothing like my father! I will not have another madman for the second chapter of my life! If my mother had been raised like I was raised, among good healthy fun-loving, hard-working people, instead of that House of Usher she escaped in Indiana, she never woulda married a maniac like my father!

ELLIE.   But your father's done very well.

LUCILLE.   At the expense of practically everybody in the Western World.

ELLIE.   And your mother's still married to him.

LUCILLE.   Well, they worked it out. Finally.

ELLIE.   *Exactement.*

LUCILLE.   He should kneel down and thank God for her.

ELLIE.   Maybe he does.

LUCILLE.   It's unlikely. It'd make him shorter.

ELLIE.   You've got to think of this as an opportunity.

LUCILLE.   An opportunity to what?

ELLIE.   Do you have an open mind?

LUCILLE.   It's open. But it ain't off the hinge.

ELLIE.   Listen to me, Lucille. You can make this work.

LUCILLE.   I should've married that osteopath Daddy hated.

ELLIE.   Listen. I don't think you want to marry John Wayne, Lucille. I think you want to be John Wayne!

LUCILLE.   Huh?

ELLIE.   I'll go further. I think you *are* John Wayne!

LUCILLE.   Huh?

ELLIE.   I mean, if I had to choose, cast, from the casting pool of you and Arthur, the role of John Wayne, that's you! You've got the part! Arthur's like, I don't know, Walter Brennan, Gabby Hayes, but no way is he The Duke! That's you! No! You know who Arthur is? Maureen O'Hara! Maureen O'Hara in *The Quiet Man.* Perfect!

LUCILLE.   Arthur is Maureen O'Hara?

ELLIE.   That's right. He set up a situation, he's in a jam! You can't consummate your marriage. Don't you get it? *You're* supposed to save Arthur! He's waiting to see. You're not supposed to stay home and blow your nose and wait for news. This bizarre evil psychiatrist character has stolen Arthur's socks. I mean, the set-up is there! Arthur is testing you! Or probably better yet, Arthur is fulfilling your prophecy, the reason that you chose Arthur! You're too strong, Lucille! You're too beautiful and too strong and too smart to stay home while somebody else goes out and kicks down the door between you and a vigorous marriage!

LUCILLE.   Arthur is Maureen O'Hara?

ELLIE.   Think of it this way. If you already knew what your marriage to Arthur will be, you might as well not marry him! It's boring to know! So you're getting pushed into this situation from a funny angle. That's interesting! Maybe your husband-to-be's a sexual deviant. So what? What's the harm?

LUCILLE.   But you're telling me Arthur's impotent!

ELLIE.   Well, you're going to have to get those socks back. That goes without saying. It falls to you. Arthur tried to get 'em, Howard tried to get 'em. I'd go, but who the hell am I?

LUCILLE.   The thing that spooks me to the bone is who the hell is Arthur?! He's a different man than I thought he was!

ELLIE.   He is different, but so what?

LUCILLE.   I thought I knew what story I was in, but if this is the story, I don't know it. And I don't know how it turns out.

ELLIE.   So that means it's a real story. Not just one you're telling. It's one that's being told from out there to you, and you're hearing it for the first time. *(The intercom buzzer rings.)*

LUCILLE.   Who's that? It's the dressmaker. She's Norwegian. *(Answers the intercom.) Ga donka day.* Hi. Come on up. *(Hangs up, says to Ellie.)* It's Arthur! He's coming up!

ELLIE.   Should I go? I should go.

LUCILLE.   Help me out of this dress! It's bad luck! *(Ellie helps Lucille, who's wearing a strapless white bodysuit underneath.)*

ELLIE.   Did you know he was coming?.

LUCILLE.   No.

ELLIE.   Is there a back door to this place by any chance?

LUCILLE.   No, and it's too far to jump. I'm afraid you're trapped in the bottle with the bee. *(A knock comes at the door.)*

Coming! Stow it in the closet, would you?

ELLIE.   My God, I wish I had your figure!

LUCILLE.   I like it. Where's that beer?! *(Takes a slug, puts it down.)* Fortified. Come in, Arthur, the door's open. *(Arthur enters. He's wearing mildly paint-spattered clothes and a leather jacket over them. He's in an emotional state.)*

ARTHUR.   Lucille! I've got to talk to you. What are you wearing?

LUCILLE.   I'm Victoria's Secret. Peek-a-boo!

ARTHUR.   Yes. Lucille, I've got to talk to you. You're not alone. Hello, Ellie.

ELLIE.   Hello, Arthur.

LUCILLE.   Excuse my appearance. I had my wedding gown on. It's supposed to be bad luck ... *(But she stops speaking.)*

ELLIE.   Should I leave? I could leave. I'll leave.

ARTHUR.   No. Stay. Maybe it's better this way. All my life ... *(He suppresses a cry.)*

LUCILLE.   Ellie, maybe you should go.

ARTHUR.   No. Stay. All my life I've been a secretive person, Lucille, and I guess I've got to change.

LUCILLE.   Arthur.

ARTHUR.   I'm weak. I've hidden things from you. I can't believe you'd love me if you knew.

LUCILLE.   Arthur.

ARTHUR.   I didn't trust you or anybody. Now my secrets have fallen into the wrong hands and I may be destroyed.

LUCILLE.   Arthur, stop.

ARTHUR.   Please don't stop me! You don't know what it's like to be me. Nobody knows what it's like. But that's my fault. There's other things that I had no control over, but I could've been more honest at least. Taken the chance. And that's what I'm going to do. Now. Lucille, I'm a —

LUCILLE.   I know.

ARTHUR.   What?

LUCILLE.   I know. Howard told Ellie and Ellie told me.

ELLIE.   Sorry.

ARTHUR.   I don't even want you to look at me! Don't look at me. What must you think of me? What must you ...

41

LUCILLE. It's not so bad.

ARTHUR. I lied. I lied to you. And I can't make love anymore. I can't stand being seen like this!

LUCILLE. It's okay.

ARTHUR. How can it be okay?

LUCILLE. It has to be okay, doesn't it?

ARTHUR. How can that be?

LUCILLE. That's the way it is.

ARTHUR. If you can know everything about me, and love me, then I'm saved.

LUCILLE. Well, we'll see about that. First things first. What's the name of this psychiatrist?

ARTHUR. Dr. Block.

LUCILLE. You want me to go to him for you, don't you?

ARTHUR. I would never ask you to, but would you?

LUCILLE. I'll go.

ARTHUR. Are you sure?

LUCILLE. Yes, but I feel like I don't know you now.

ARTHUR. The real truth is though that you didn't know me before. I'm sorry I deceived you. Habit of a lifetime. I'm sorry. *(Kneels down.)* And I beg your forgiveness. Forgive me. Forgive me.

ELLIE. Lucy.

LUCILLE. You give me too much power.

ARTHUR. No. You have this power. Please. Forgive me.

ELLIE. Southern light's the best light, Lucy. Everybody knows that. Northern light is steady. Southern light changes all the time, but everybody wants their light from the South.

LUCILLE. I forgive you, Arthur.

ELLIE. Lucy. Yes.

LUCILLE. Stand up, be a man, and I'll love you.

ARTHUR. I don't know if I can.

LUCILLE. Yes you can. *(Kisses him heartily. Finishes. Wipes away the kiss.)* All right! Yes. Well! And now for Dr. Block!

BLACKOUT

Scene 2

Dr. Block's office. The same as before, except now there's a vase of sunflowers.

Dr. Block is on the phone.

BLOCK.   All the Greek Islands. Oh, I'll go for the suite. With a nice window. Two. Leeward side of the ship. Good. *(A knock on the door.)* Hold on. *(Calls.)* Come in. *(Back to the phone.)* Peter says what? *(Lucille comes in. She's wearing a lovely suit. Block waves to her pleasantly and wraps up his call.)* That's fine. I'll walk the deposit over to you later. Thanks, Jeff. Thank you. *(He hangs up the phone.)*

LUCILLE.   Dr. Block?

BLOCK.   Lucille? Your picture doesn't do you justice. Call me Henry.

LUCILLE.   I prefer to call you Doctor, thanks.

BLOCK.   As you please. Make yourself comfortable.

LUCILLE.   Those flowers.

BLOCK.   Sunflowers. Your favorite, right?

LUCILLE.   I forget. You know a lot about me.

BLOCK.   Well, you've been filled in about me, too, right?

LUCILLE.   Right.

BLOCK.   But did you know that I'm the founder of the Psychiatric Syndicalist Movement?

LUCILLE.   No, I didn't.

BLOCK.   I should add that I'm the founder and the only member.

LUCILLE.   How much do you charge?

BLOCK.   The philosophy of the Movement is, when it comes to the patient, all the force necessary.

LUCILLE.   What made you start a movement with no one in it but you?

BLOCK.   Psychiatric Syndicalism would be a disaster if it was actually practiced for any length of time by anybody. It presumes a ruthless certainty that I know something and you don't. It's a kind of emotional fascism. I only cooked it up for Arthur.

LUCILLE. For my Arthur?

BLOCK. Let's say eighty dollars for the session. *(She immediately holds out a bill.)*

LUCILLE. Cheap! Well, you get what you pay for. Can you break a hundred? *(He takes the bill.)*

BLOCK. I see that you're trying to set a certain tone. *(He gets a twenty out of his wallet and hands it over.)*

LUCILLE. Where I come from we pay our bills. *(She sits.)*

BLOCK. Arthur suffers from a horrible paternalistic scar. As do many men, in different ways.

LUCILLE. He showed you my picture?

BLOCK. Oh yes.

LUCILLE. What did you think?

BLOCK. I thought, you're a beautiful woman.

LUCILLE. You're damn right I am. But that's not all I am. He mentioned I like the sunflowers?

BLOCK. Yes.

LUCILLE. Mentioning's one thing, you going out and buying a bunch is another. It's not very doctorly.

BLOCK. That's true.

LUCILLE. Maybe I shouldn't have come.

BLOCK. Oh, you had to come!

LUCILLE. It couldn't be that you've set your cap for me?

BLOCK. In a way. *(She stands.)* Sit down! I said, sit down! *(She continues to stand.)*

LUCILLE. I don't care what you said.

BLOCK. You know Arthur's friend Howard?

LUCILLE. You know I do.

BLOCK. It's an unequal friendship where Arthur was held down by Howard. Howard wanted to lord it over somebody, some MAN, to assuage his own damaged self-esteem. Arthur willingly was that man. This is what men do to each other. It makes me sick.

LUCILLE. Me too. *(She sits.)*

BLOCK. First Arthur's father usurped his manhood, then other men who fit the bill filled the role. Arthur's only known competition and cruelty from men, and yet he needs to be a man and to be sexually competent.

LUCILLE.   That is the pickle.

BLOCK.   I can give you back the socks, but ...

LUCILLE.   I want the socks.

BLOCK.   But it won't exactly solve the problem.

LUCILLE.   I'm not leaving here without the socks.

BLOCK.   So you heard about how I held the socks out to Howard and convinced him not to take them out of my hand?

LUCILLE.   Yes. *(Block laughs.)*

BLOCK.   That was good!

LUCILLE.   Was it?

BLOCK.   But! The fix was in. I knew Howard didn't really want to help Arthur. Howard doesn't really want to help any man. But you, Lucille, you're different.

LUCILLE.   You're not going to snow me, Doctor.

BLOCK.   You see, the only hope for most men is women. The feminine antidote. That's why I'm quitting the business.

LUCILLE.   Why don't you just give them to me?

BLOCK.   Patience! I've had to be patient! Six years I've been trying to cure Arthur of a simple fetish, and I haven't been able to do it. Six years! Seven hundred and ninety-seven fruitless sessions. So finally, I started my movement, my resolve to violate my own ethics. I conned Arthur into bringing in the socks, and I stole them! I JUST COULDN'T BRING MYSELF TO LET HIM GO AND GET MARRIED WITH THOSE SOCKS! Call me unethical, unscrupulous, a crackpot! Whatever you call me, I've called myself worse! My only defense is I swore I'd quit the business if I could cure this one man. And I can cure him! I will cure him! But of course I can't cure him! Alone.

LUCILLE.   Well, you are a piece of work, aren't you?

BLOCK.   I am driven by obscure propulsions of my own, my dear. Arthur was driven to Art. This is my Art. Arthur is my subject, and I must get him right! And I can! But only through you.

LUCILLE.   What's your point?

BLOCK.   You are beautiful. I am charmed. Arthur is fortunate.

LUCILLE.   Thank you. What's your point, Dr. Block?

BLOCK.   What's your relationship with your mother and father?

LUCILLE.   It'll do.

BLOCK.   You don't care to talk about it?

LUCILLE.   I'm not going to talk about it! I'm not going to vary from my purpose here. You know what I think? I think that Arthur beat you at your own game. I think anybody takes this job you've got likes to sit behind the glass and feel smug. Something in Arthur beat you four-square and completely. Six years of trying and you came up empty and you can't live with it! So now you've broken your own rules and reached across the legal line and snatched his socks! He sees that as you having the strength, but I see it for what it is. Defeat. He has defeated you. So now you're trying one last gambit, somehow, through me, to ace him. Well, good luck!

BLOCK.   I never get people like you in my office.

LUCILLE.   No surprise there.

BLOCK.   Not that I shouldn't.

LUCILLE.   You're pitiful. You're like an old dog don't wanna get off the foot of the bed. You oughta get out more.

BLOCK.   I intend to.

LUCILLE.   Don't wait too long. Give me the socks, Block.

BLOCK.   You don't like me?

LUCILLE.   No.

BLOCK.   You don't like my company?

LUCILLE.   You're not company. I don't pay for company. And if I did pay for company, you ain't it.

BLOCK.   What don't you like about me?

LUCILLE.   You're boring.

BLOCK.   You're seeing me within a certain context.

LUCILLE.   I see you fine. You're a gold-plated snooze.

BLOCK.   Heard it all before, seen it all before, eh?

LUCILLE.   No sir. I wouldn't do this twice.

BLOCK.   You are beautiful.

LUCILLE.   More beautiful than you'll ever know, Frankenstein. You can kiss my foot.

BLOCK.   How can you say that? You don't even know me.

LUCILLE.   I'm a witch. *(Smiles.)* You're a certain brand of ballbreaker and a very particular kind of lech. I have a sister in Michigan who might fall for your jabber, but even she probably couldn't get past your mediocre looks. If you want to streetfight with me, baby, you'd better get yourself a knife. Now I suggest, before I say something that sticks in your bile duct for the rest of your life, you surrender the footwear!

BLOCK. A fabulous macho display.

LUCILLE. You should see me sit a horse.

BLOCK. I'm sure you would dominate.

LUCILLE. You think there's something wrong with me?

BLOCK. Yes.

LUCILLE. You say what it is.

BLOCK. All right, I will. Where is the yielding side of you, Lucille?

LUCILLE. In my closet. With many pairs of shoes.

BLOCK. Where's the softness, the silence? Where's a man to lay his head with you stomping around like the world was your bunkhouse and you were a spur-jangling buckaroo? You took after your father. You took after him a long time ago, but you'll never catch him. The degree to which you succeed in being your father is that exact degree to which you shall fail in your womanhood.

LUCILLE. Are you saying I'm not a woman?!

BLOCK. You've got a ways to go.

LUCILLE. Why you…. You are not a gentleman!

BLOCK. But enough. I didn't bring you here for treatment. The curtain rises. Lucille, do you want to run off with me, take a cruise to Greece? The islands are beautiful I hear.

LUCILLE. Are you serious?

BLOCK. Yes.

LUCILLE. Are you crazy?

BLOCK. Probably. But I'm getting out of the racket. I can do what I want. What's your answer?

LUCILLE. No!

BLOCK. Please reconsider!

LUCILLE. No!

BLOCK. You're sure? This is a real offer now.

LUCILLE. Yes, I'm sure! Have you been dippin' into the

pharmaceuticals there, Henry?!

BLOCK.   Now stop! Very good! This was a scene and the scene is over. The curtain falls.

LUCILLE.   Don't touch me!

BLOCK.   Be quiet! I have not the slightest biological interest in you. Attend me. Your happiness and a man's true health are in the balance. Do what I tell you. Tell Arthur I bought you the flowers, commented on your beauty. Tell Arthur I asked you to run away with me. But you never wavered.

LUCILLE.   You mean? What do you mean?

BLOCK.   Do what I tell you.

LUCILLE.   You mean you wanted me to turn you down?

BLOCK.   Even if I had succeeded in curing this man of his fetish, he still would've been in the power of a man. That was my dilemma right along. He still would've owed his manhood to a man. His problem would've remained, at root, the same. No. His salvation is woman. You.

LUCILLE.   Forgive Salvation for being slow, but am I to pull together from this that you are a good guy?

BLOCK.   That's right. I am a good guy.

LUCILLE.   That sticks in my craw.

BLOCK.   You marry. My prediction: Six months, his need for the fetish dissolves. Here are the socks. Have a wonderful honeymoon.

LUCILLE.   IF I marry. Keep the gall-blamed socks, I'll be damned.

BLOCK.   What do you mean, IF you marry? You've got to marry him. What's your reservation?

LUCILLE.   You.

BLOCK.   Me? What do I have to do with it?

LUCILLE.   I don't wanna do a damn thing you want me to do.

BLOCK.   Why not?

LUCILLE.   You're impolite.

BLOCK.   You're not serious.

LUCILLE.   Why should I please you after you bad-mouthed me?

BLOCK.   Because I'm right.

LUCILLE.   That answer lacks charm. You have mortally insulted my femininity and I am not going to do anything you want, INCLUDING MARRYING ARTHUR, until you mend that fence.

BLOCK. What do you mean? An apology?

LUCILLE. You're gonna have to do better than that. I am beautiful, I am charming, Arthur is fortunate. Make me believe it!

BLOCK. What do you want me to say?

LUCILLE. I don't know. You broke it, you fix it.

BLOCK. You mean speak in a complimentary way about your ...

LUCILLE. With conviction.

BLOCK. What if I don't have conviction?

LUCILLE. You've got it.

BLOCK. So you feel certain that I have some actual ...

LUCILLE. That's right, Egghead! Admit it! Your body temperature's been all over Laredo since my perfume took over this room! Just 'cause I stomp around a little bit don't mean I ain't a dewy little thing. Do you feel me in this room or not?

BLOCK. Yes, but ...

LUCILLE. Then say something to pluff me up to where I was when I walked into this office, or the wedding is off!

BLOCK. All right. You look good.

LUCILLE. People say that about the dead.

BLOCK. You have a nice forehead.

LUCILLE. Shakespeare can sleep tonight.

BLOCK. All right. I wish I could kiss you.

LUCILLE. That's better but you can't!

BLOCK. I have no desire to!

LUCILLE. Strike two!

BLOCK. You're oxymoronic!

LUCILLE. But I'm supposed to be IRRESISTIBLE! Now maybe these men patients you get need to be abused, but I am a woman AND BY GOD I NEED AFFIRMATION!

BLOCK. Very well. You're a charismatic, deeply fetching woman. Every minute with you is poignant torture because I am racked with jealousy that Arthur gets you and I don't.

LUCILLE. Much better!

BLOCK. I feel like you've taken my senses to the rodeo.

LUCILLE. Okay, I'm satisfied.

BLOCK. I feel roped and thrown and unable to free my horns from the grip of attraction.

LUCILLE. I believe you.

BLOCK. I wish I'd met you in some other world, unfettered by obligation and history.

LUCILLE. The curtain falls!

BLOCK. And I must once, to honor and acknowledge something in myself, hold you in my arms and blow on your hair! *(Block picks her up and blows on her hair. Lucille reacts to this by yelling.)*

LUCILLE. Help! *(The door flies open. It's Arthur and Howard.)*

ARTHUR. LUCY!

LUCILLE. ARTHUR!

HOWARD. BLOCK!

ARTHUR. I knew it. Put her down! *(Block drops Lucille on the couch.)*

BLOCK. I can explain!

HOWARD. Oh no you don't! No more talking!

ARTHUR. Are you all right?

LUCILLE. Yes, Arthur. You saved me!

ARTHUR. I guess I did.

BLOCK. I can explain.

HOWARD. None of your tricks, Svengali!

ARTHUR. GIVE ME THOSE SOCKS!

BLOCK. Very well. *(Block hands the socks to Arthur. Arthur hands them to Lucille.)*

ARTHUR. Hold these for me, will you?

LUCILLE. Sure thing, sweetie.

ARTHUR. Don't you ever take anybody's socks again.

HOWARD. And I was the Roman in the dream! *(Arthur has been locked in a loving gaze with Lucille.)*

ARTHUR. I didn't want you alone with him.

LUCILLE. Why not?

ARTHUR. Because I love you! *(They kiss. The kiss ends.)*

LUCILLE. Arthur.

ARTHUR. Yeah?

LUCILLE.   I am fortunate.

ARTHUR.   Six years. Come on. Let's get out of here.

HOWARD.   That's fine with me. This place gives me the willies.

BLOCK.   Wait! I want to explain.

LUCILLE.   Make it quick.

BLOCK.   All right. I will. I'm a man.

LUCILLE.   A word of advice. Don't try and hide behind your penis. It won't provide enough cover. *(Now she addresses Arthur and Howard.)* Come on, boys! I'm getting married! Here comes the Bride! *(They go. The Wedding March begins to play. Block gets up and dusts himself off.)*

BLOCK.   797 sessions. Case closed. *(Distant bells are heard.)* Ahh. Wedding bells. That old familiar theme. Man and woman. The archetypal picture. Society refrains from the ordinary and returns to the grand ritual.

LUCILLE'S VOICE.   Ellie! Ellie! *(Block disappears. Arthur and Howard float into view in silhouette, dressing and singing.)*

ARTHUR and HOWARD.

> Buffalo gal won't you come out tonight?
>
> Won't you come out tonight?
>
> Won't you come out tonight?
>
> Buffalo gal won't you come out tonight,
>
> And dance by the light of the moon?

(They disappear.)

ELLIE.   *(Entering.)* I have the bouquet! I have the bouquet! I am the maid of honor and I have the bouquet! *(Lucille enters.)* Sunflowers. In the best sense of the word, you look perfect.

ARTHUR.   *(Enters in a tuxedo.)* Lucille! Did you get the socks?

LUCILLE.   I've got 'em, baby!

ARTHUR.   Saved by the Texas belle! Where's my best man? *(Enter Howard, also in a tux.)*

HOWARD.   Right here! This is intimacy. We are friends, aren't we?

ARTHUR.   Sure we are. You got the ring?

HOWARD.   Got it! *(Block, who has become the minister, enters.)*

BLOCK.   We are gathered together ...

LUCILLE.   We certainly are.

ELLIE.   God, you're beautiful!

BLOCK.   To celebrate the holy sacrament of matrimony ...

ARTHUR.   Lucy, the socks?

BLOCK.   Will you take this woman?

ARTHUR.   Yes.

BLOCK.   Will you take this man?

LUCILLE.   Yes.

ARTHUR.   Lucy, the socks?

LUCILLE.   What will you give me for them?

ARTHUR.   Howard, the ring! *(Howard gives Arthur the ring.)*

HOWARD.   Presto.

ARTHUR.   I'll give you this ring.

LUCILLE.   It's a deal! *(She hands him the socks. He stuffs them in his pocket and places the ring on her finger.)*

ARTHUR.   With this ring ...

LUCILLE and ARTHUR.   I thee wed.

BLOCK.

> And so I officiate
> And bring to conclusion
> This tale of love
> And a lover's delusion
>
> But I ask you to note
> As you laugh and dismiss
> The terms of this fellow's
> Relation to bliss
>
> We all of us need
> Some yeast in the bread
> To link up the heart
> And the soul and the head
>
> So forgive him
> His foolish fantastic connection
> It's a roundabout road
> 'Tween sex and affection!

ALL.   Amen. *(The music swells.)*

THE END

PROPERTY LIST

Coffee cups with coffee (ELLIE, HOWARD)
Pad and pen or pencil (ELLIE)
The Wall St. Journal newspaper (HOWARD)
Remote control device (ELLIE)
Old pair of argyle socks (BLOCK, LUCILLE)
Gavel (BLOCK)
Banana (LUCILLE)
Tea (LUCILLE)
Beer (LUCILLE)
$100 bill (LUCILLE)
Wallet with $20 bill (BLOCK)
Bouquet of flowers (ELLIE)
Wedding ring (HOWARD)

SOUND EFFECTS

Sweet doorbell
Intercom buzzer
Distant bells

NEW PLAYS

• MERE MORTALS by David Ives, author of *All in the Timing*. Another critically acclaimed evening of one-act comedies combining wit, satire, hilarity and intellect -- a winning combination. The entire evening of plays can be performed by 3 men and 3 women. ISBN: 0-8222-1632-9

• BALLAD OF YACHIYO by Philip Kan Gotanda. A provocative play about innocence, passion and betrayal, set against the backdrop of a Hawaiian sugar plantation in the early 1900s. *"Gotanda's writing is superb ... a great deal of fine craftsmanship on display here, and much to enjoy."* --*Variety*. *"...one of the country's most consistently intriguing playwrights..."* --*San Francisco Examiner*. *"As he has in past plays, Gotanda defies expectations..."* --*Oakland Tribune*. [3M, 4W] ISBN: 0-8222-1547-0

• MINUTES FROM THE BLUE ROUTE by Tom Donaghy. While packing up a house, a family converges for a weekend of flaring tempers and shattered illusions. *"With MINUTES FROM THE BLUE ROUTE [Donaghy] succeeds not only in telling a story -- a typically American one with wide appeal, about how parents and kids struggle to understand each other and mostly fail -- but in notating it inventively, through wittily elliptical, crisscrossed speeches, and in making it carry a fairly vast amount of serious weight with surprising ease."* --*Village Voice*. [2M, 2W] ISBN: 0-8222-1608-6

• SCAPIN by Molière, adapted by Bill Irwin and Mark O'Donnell. This adaptation of Molière's 325-year-old farce, *Les Fourberies de Scapin*, keeps the play in period while adding a late Twentieth Century spin to the language and action. *"This SCAPIN, [with a] felicitous adaptation by Mark O'Donnell, would probably have gone over big with the same audience who first saw Molière's Fourberies de Scapin...in Paris in 1671."* --*N.Y. Times*. *"Commedia dell'arte and vaudeville have at least two things in common: baggy pants and Bill Irwin. All make for a natural fit in the celebrated clown's entirely unconventional adaptation."* --*Variety* [9M, 3W, flexible] ISBN: 0-8222-1603-5

• THE TURN OF THE SCREW adapted for the stage by Jeffrey Hatcher from the story by Henry James. The American master's classic tale of possession is given its most interesting "turn" yet: one woman plays the mansion's terrified governess while a single male actor plays everyone else. *"In his thoughtful adaptation of Henry James' spooky tale, Jeffrey Hatcher does away with the supernatural flummery, exchanging the story's balanced ambiguities about the nature of reality for a portrait of psychological vampirism..."* --*Boston Globe*. [1M, 1W] ISBN: 0-8222-1554-3

• NEVILLE'S ISLAND by Tim Firth. A middle management orientation exercise turns into an hilarious disaster when the team gets "shipwrecked" on an uninhabited island. *"NEVILLE'S ISLAND ... is that rare event: a genuinely good new play..., it's a comedic, adult LORD OF THE FLIES..."* --*The Guardian*. *"... A non-stop, whitewater deluge of comedy both sophisticated and slapstick.... Firth takes a perfect premise and shoots it to the extreme, flipping his fish out of water, watching them flop around a bit, and then masterminding the inevitable feeding frenzy."* --*New Mexican*. [4M] ISBN: 0-8222-1581-0

DRAMATISTS PLAY SERVICE, INC.
440 Park Avenue South, New York, NY 10016 212-683-8960 Fax 212-213-1539
postmaster@dramatists.com www.dramatists.com

NEW PLAYS

• **TAKING SIDES by Ronald Harwood.** Based on the true story of one of the world's greatest conductors whose wartime decision to remain in Germany brought him under the scrutiny of a U.S. Army determined to prove him a Nazi. *"A brave, wise and deeply moving play delineating the confrontation between culture, and power, between art and politics, between irresponsible freedom and responsible compromise."* --*London Sunday Times.* [4M, 3W] ISBN: 0-8222-1566-7

• **MISSING/KISSING by John Patrick Shanley.** Two biting short comedies, MISSING MARISA and KISSING CHRISTINE, by one of America's foremost dramatists and the Academy Award winning author of *Moonstruck.* *" ... Shanley has an unusual talent for situations ... and a sure gift for a kind of inner dialogue in which people talk their hearts as well as their minds...."* --*N.Y. Post.* MISSING MARISA [2M], KISSING CHRISTINE [1M, 2W] ISBN: 0-8222-1590-X

• **THE SISTERS ROSENSWEIG by Wendy Wasserstein,** Pulitzer Prize-winning author of *The Heidi Chronicles.* Winner of the 1993 Outer Critics Circle Award for Best Broadway Play. A captivating portrait of three disparate sisters reuniting after a lengthy separation on the eldest's 50th birthday. *"The laughter is all but continuous."* --*New Yorker.* *"Funny. Observant. A play with wit as well as acumen.... In dealing with social and cultural paradoxes, Ms. Wasserstein is, as always, the most astute of commentators."* --*N.Y. Times.* [4M, 4W] ISBN: 0-8222-1348-6

• **MASTER CLASS by Terrence McNally. Winner of the 1996 Tony Award for Best Play.** Only a year after winning the Tony Award for *Love! Valour! Compassion!,* Terrence McNally scores again with the most celebrated play of the year, an unforgettable portrait of Maria Callas, our century's greatest opera diva. *"One of the white-hot moments of contemporary theatre. A total triumph."* --*N.Y. Post.* *"Blazingly theatrical."* -- *USA Today.* [3M, 3W] ISBN: 0-8222-1521-7

• **DEALER'S CHOICE by Patrick Marber.** A weekly poker game pits a son addicted to gambling against his own father, who also has a problem but won't admit it. *"... make tracks to DEALER'S CHOICE, Patrick Marber's wonderfully masculine, razor-sharp dissection of poker-as-life.... It's a play that comes out swinging and never lets up -- a witty, wisecracking drama that relentlessly probes the tortured souls of its six very distinctive ... characters. CHOICE is a cutthroat pleasure that you won't want to miss."* --*Time Out (New York).* [6M] ISBN: 0-8222-1616-7

• **RIFF RAFF by Laurence Fishburne.** RIFF RAFF marks the playwriting debut of one of Hollywood's most exciting and versatile actors. *"Mr. Fishburne is surprisingly and effectively understated, with scalding bubbles of anxiety breaking through the surface of a numbed calm."* --*N.Y. Times.* *"Fishburne has a talent and a quality...[he] possesses one of the vital requirements of a playwright -- a good ear for the things people say and the way they say them."* --*N.Y. Post.* [3M] ISBN: 0-8222-1545-4

DRAMATISTS PLAY SERVICE, INC.
440 Park Avenue South, New York, NY 10016 212-683-8960 Fax 212-213-1539
postmaster@dramatists.com www.dramatists.com